1

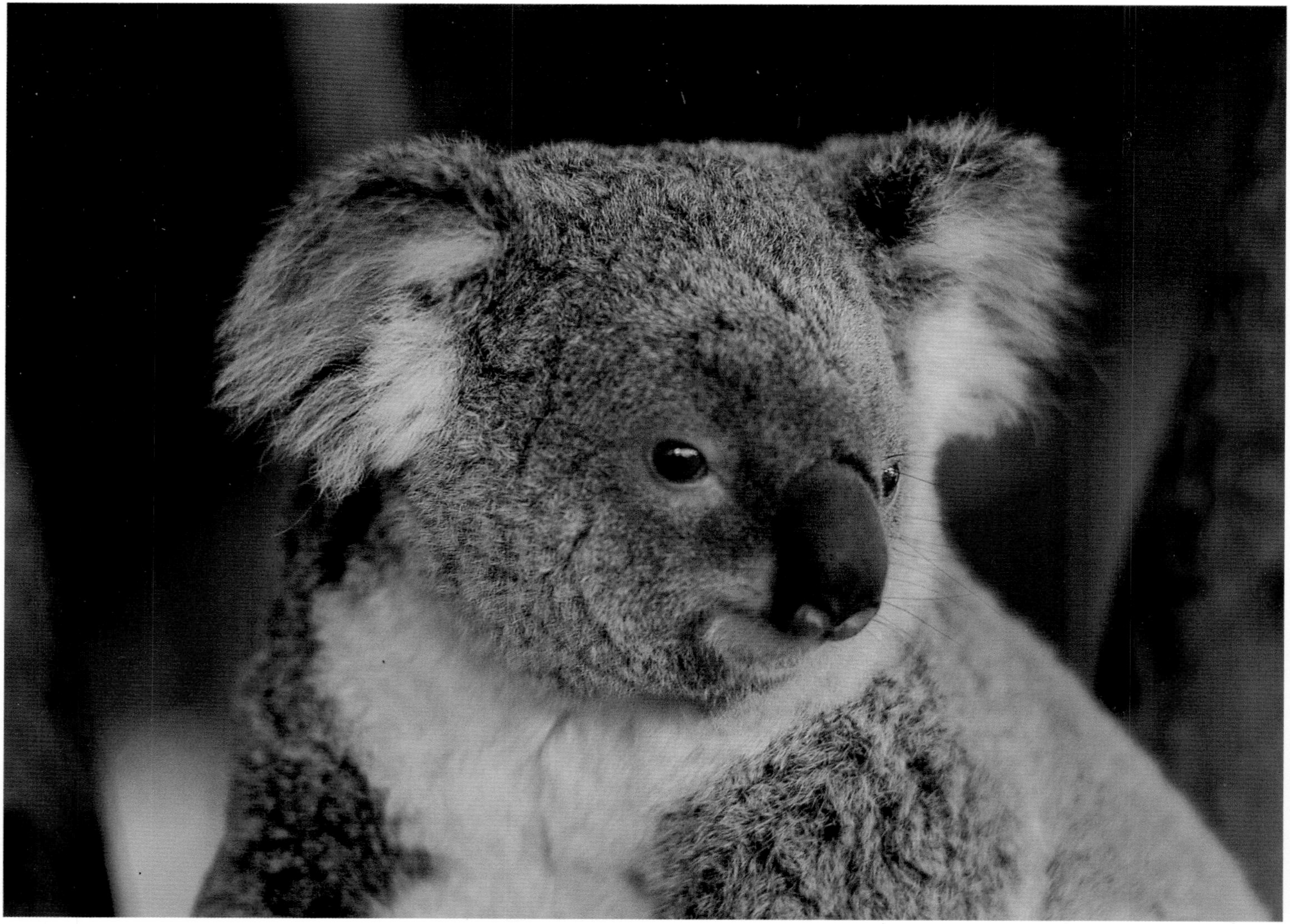

KOALAS

Sleepy and cute, the koala is Australia's real-life answer to the teddy bear. Spending only about five hours awake each day, that's enough time for an adult still to chew through a kilo of leaves. Their docile habits make koalas hard to spot in the wild. Only in 1798, 10 years after the First Fleet arrived at Sydney Town, did the European settlers report encountering an animal 'which the natives call a cullawine'. At first, the settlers called the animals sloths or monkeys, until Aboriginal words were blended into 'koala'. Koalas are marsupials, that is, they have pouches and their newborn are small and sightless. After birth, the young crawls through its mother's fur and into her pouch; once a little older, it rides on its mother's back. The koala is most commonly found in Queensland, but also lives in New South Wales, Victoria and the ACT.

WALLABIES

Wallabies are much like kangaroos, except smaller. Plus wallabies have shorter feet. The brush-tailed rock wallaby has a vast habitat that extends from mountainous, forested coastal regions to caves and crevices in more arid regions. Other varieties include the swamp wallaby, found in marshy country and on hillsides, and the spectacled hare-wallaby, which has an attractive orange ring around its eyes.

KANGAROOS

Kangaroos are marsupials, which means their babies, called joeys, are born tiny and blind. After birth, the joey crawls into its mother's pouch and attaches itself to one of her teats. Kangaroos are herbivores, meaning they eat leaves, berries, roots and grasses. They use their muscly hind legs to hop at high speed and their long, strong tails for balance. When standing still or moving slowly, a kangaroo uses its tail like a third leg. Kangaroos are a very diverse group, ranging from the tall, fast variety of the open plains (such as red kangaroos) to tree-kangaroos. Then there's rat-kangaroos, who look more like bandicoots than roos. By the way, the red kangaroo is the world's largest marsupial and Australia's largest native mammal.

DINGOS

The dingo is one dog whose bark isn't worse than its bite. The dingo, you see, howls, yes, but never barks. Australia's only native dog, the dingo arrived in Australia about 8,000 to 10,000 years ago, hitching a ride with a relatively recent wave of migrating Aborigines who kept the animals as pets. The dingo's closest relative is probably the plains wolf of India. Much as rabbits and foxes did thousands of years later, the dingo soon established a 'feral' existence apart from its Aboriginal masters.

ECHIDNAS

The echidna, or spiny ant-eater, has survived remarkably well since the arrival of Europeans in 1788. When attacked, an echidna digs its sharp claws into the ground, becoming virtually impossible to dislodge. Related to the platypus (both are egg-laying monotremes), the echidna is a primitive mammal whose long, fast, sticky tongue is perfect for seeking out ants, termites and other small insects. During breeding season, the female develops a temporary pouch, into which she lays a soft-shelled egg. She incubates the egg until the youngster forms spines, then she hides her offspring in a burrow.

TASMANIAN DEVIL

Following the extinction of the Thylacine, or *'Tasmanian tiger'*, Australia's largest carnivore is the Tasmanian devil. Despite its name and aggressive appearance, however, the Tasmanian devil is no hunter. Instead, its strong jaws and razor-sharp teeth are perfectly evolved for devouring carrion (dead animals). The devil once lived on mainland Australia, but last century land clearing for agriculture forced the devil to retreat into rugged patches of Tasmanian hinterland. For a while, the devil was endangered, but now numbers are secure. The devil's closest relative is the native cat, with whom it shares the habit of carefully licking a paw before using it to wash his face.

WOMBATS

The wombat is the ground-dwelling relative of the koala. Sharp, long claws and short, strong forearms make wombats expert diggers: they create extensive burrow systems where they shelter during the day. At night they emerge to feed on roots, leaves and grasses. The common wombat, found in coastal forests of the south-eastern mainland and Tasmania, can weigh up to 35 kgs but rarely exceeds a metre in length. The hairy-nosed wombat, found in arid coastal and inland regions of Western Australia and South Australia, can go without water for three or four months, enduring the heat by lowering its metabolic rate and sleeping in interconnecting burrows during the day.

EMUS

Of Australia's two large flightless native birds, the emu and the cassowary, the emu is much better known, although for many years it was actually known as the New Holland or New South Wales cassowary. As well as figuring prominently in Aboriginal folklore, the emu retains symbolic significance because during World War I Australian cavalrymen attached emu plumes to their slouch hats. In much of Australia, wild emu numbers have fallen drastically, but in Western Australia they continue to thrive, so much so that in 1932 an army machine-gun unit was sent out to cull a swelling population who were ravaging wheat crops. This bizarre, largely unsuccessful escapade was known as the Emu War.

NUMBATS

The numbat is a marsupial ant-eater with attractive, striped markings whose habitat has been largely destroyed by rabbits and foxes. It can be found only in wandoo eucalypt forests in inland Western Australia. A solitary animal, the numbat is an unusual marsupial because it has no pouch and because it is active during the day, when it forages for its favourite delicacy, termites. When it finds a nest, the numbat digs rapidly and licks up the insects with its long, sticky tongue. The numbat has also mastered an unusual escape technique: when cornered in a log it can swell its muscly rump to plug the entrance.

NOCTURNAL FEEDERS

The Australian bush, and even Australia's suburbs, become busy at night as a host of nocturnal natives search for food. One nocturnal feeder is the sugar glider, which is only about 40 cms long but can glide up to 50 metres. The sugar glider lives in forests on the northern and eastern mainland and in Tasmania; the larger squirrel glider lives in eucalypt forests in coastal regions. Bandicoots have a broader diet that includes meat: after sleeping all day under a well-built nest, they forage for worms and insect larvae at night. Other nightfeeders include the quoll, the dunnart, the antechinus, the bettong, the potoroo and the bilby, a desert-dwelling creature with cute, large ears.

15

16

GOANNAS

Australia has a staggering wealth of lizard varieties, and goannas, or monitors, grow the biggest. And biggest of all is the perentie, which can grow to over two metres. Second largest is the lace monitor, which feeds on insects, reptiles, small mammals, birds and carrion and which can run up the trunk of a tree if startled. One of the most prominent animals of Aboriginal folklore, goannas have loose, coarse skin, extended necks and bodies and forked tongues they flick to pick up 'scents'.

PARROTS

Australia's parrots and cockatoos are colourful and diverse. Probably the best known is the sulphur-crested cockatoo (above), with its shrill, piercing cry. Also known as the white cockatoo, it is common throughout northern, eastern and south-eastern Australia, including Tasmania. When in open country, sulphur-crested cockatoos have a sentinel system: while the flock feeds on the ground, a handful of guards keep watch from the treetops, squawking at any sign of an intruder. A nomadic bird found in forests, farmland, orchards, parks and gardens, the musk lorikeet (right) feeds throughout the day on pollen and nectar, while king parrots (opposite) are usually seen in pairs or small parties nibbling at the outermost branches of acacias and eucalypts.

WATERBIRDS

Australia's only stork, the jabiru (above), eats fish, reptiles, frogs, crabs, rodents and carrion. Jabirus hunt independently, striding through shallow water and foraging with their bills. Both male and female build the nest and help incubate the eggs. The jabiru is found along Australia's north and east coasts, sometimes as far south as Sydney, while the pied heron (right) lives only in the swamps and grassland of the north. It feeds primarily on insects and occasionally forages at sewage ponds and garbage tips. Pied herons lay three or four eggs in platform nests made of sticks and twigs in trees and mangroves.

BUSHBIRDS

The laughing kookaburra (left), the largest kingfisher, uses its laugh to mark out its territory. At dusk in the woodland and open forests kookaburras laugh and then await the reply of a neighbouring group. One Aboriginal legend has it that the kookaburra's laughter in the morning signalled the sky people to light the fire that warms and illuminates the world. Imitating the laugh was taboo, or else the offended sky people might condemn the world to eternal darkness. The bustard (above), used to be common. Like every other of the world's 22 species of bustards, however, the bustard's habitat (it lives in open country) has been overtaken by human settlers. Bustards are nomadic and the male has an impressive mating display, spreading his feathers and inflating his neck.

GECKOS

Found everywhere in Australia except Tasmania, geckos have the ability to shed their tails when in danger. Adapted to distract predators, the tail continues to wriggle once detached. Happily, it doesn't take the gecko long to grow a new tail. All geckos have soft bodies, and many have adhesive discs on their toes which enable them to scale walls and saunter across ceilings. While the thick-tailed gecko (above) has bright, spotted markings, the southern leaf-tailed gecko (left) has adapted to blend into its environment, helping it to elude predators.

LIZARDS

In diversity of size, form and colour, lizards probably outdo every other group of Australian fauna. Apart from goannas and geckos, there are skinks, which, with over 150 recorded species, are the most numerous lizard family. Both the thorny devil (below), which is actually a harmless desert-dwelling ant-eater, and frilled lizard (right) are dragons. The only lizard family unique to the Australian region are the pygopods, or legless lizards.

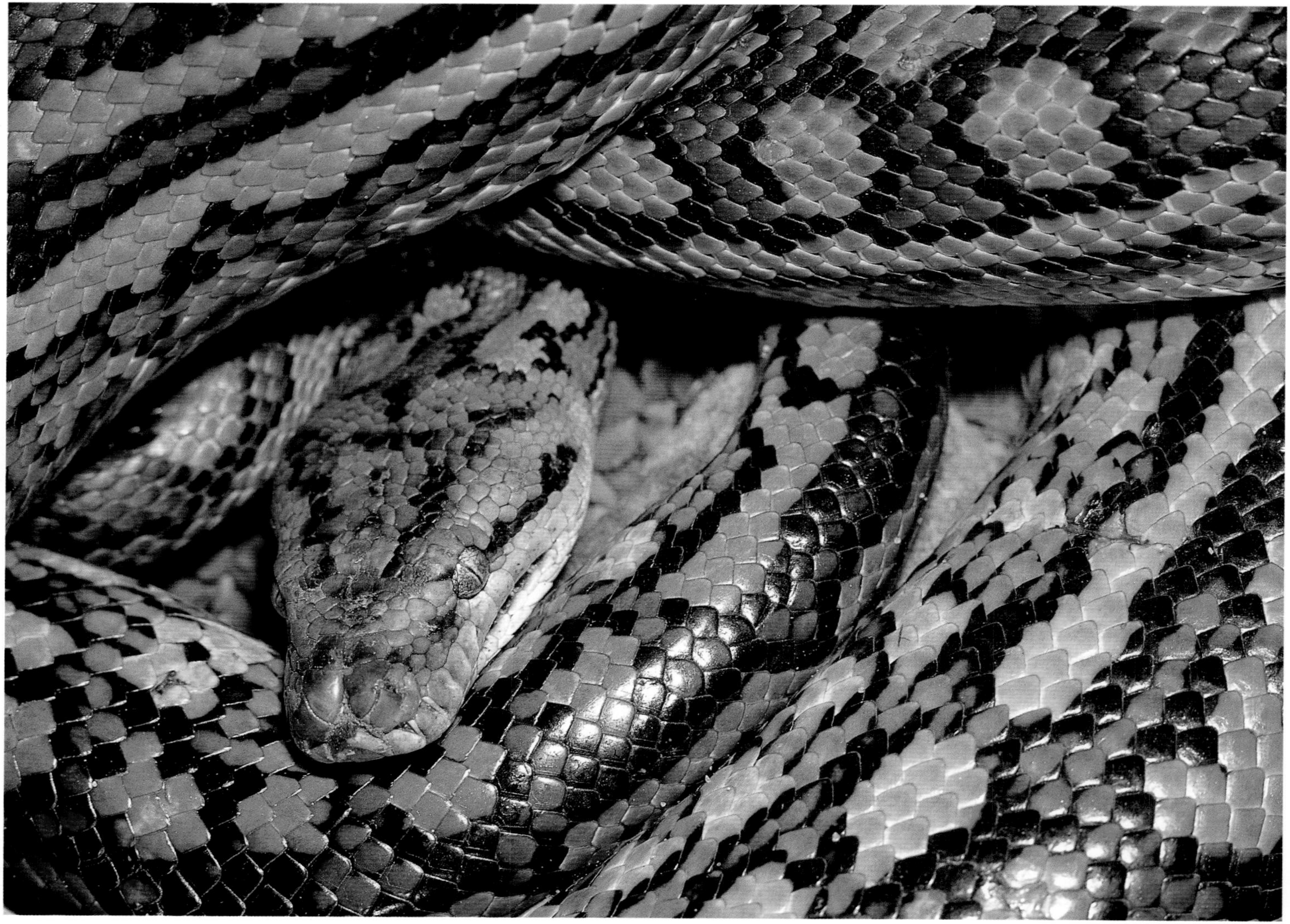

SNAKES

Australia has about 160 snake species and two-thirds of them are venomous, although only about 20 species are dangerous to humans. Five families of land snakes are found in Australia, but only three are well-represented: elapid snakes, pythons and blind snakes. The elapids include all the dangerous varieties, such as the taipan, death adder, tiger snake, copperhead, eastern brown snake and mulga snake. Snakes usually only bite humans in self-defence; the much-feared tiger snake, for instance, prefers to eat frogs and tadpoles. Unlike their venomous cousins, pythons kill prey by squeezing it until it can't breathe.

SEALS

Many aquatic mammals swim in Australian waters, among them most of the Antarctic seals. Three species of seal breed on Australian beaches — sea lions, Australian fur seals and New Zealand fur seals; while Southern elephant seals, leopard seals, Weddell seals and crab-eater seals only stop in to visit. Only recently have numbers started to recover from heavy sealing last century, when the noisy, bulky animals were harvested for fur and oil. Growing up to two metres long, the Australian fur seal can dive to a depth of 150 metres and eats squid, octopus, lobster and fish.

PLATYPUS AND TORTOISE

A monotreme, the platypus is a shy mammal that still has characteristics in common with its reptile ancestors: its skeletal structure, its egg-laying abilities and the way it has only one external opening for both reproduction and excretion (hence the name monotreme). Unlike reptiles, the platypus is warm-blooded, living in quiet creeks and mountain streams where it uses its duck-bill to forage for crustaceans and molluscs. Also in the quiet waterways you might find a carnivourous long-neck or snake-neck tortoise. Australia has two tortoise groups, the other being the short-necked, omnivorous variety. The latter sometimes live in and around fast-flowing streams and rivers.

CROCODILES

The crocodile is Australia's largest reptile, but not all crocodiles are man-eaters. Freshwater crocs are mostly harmless, even though they can grow up to 2.5 metres in length. With their long, pointy snouts their diet consists of insects, shrimp, crab and fish. More dangerous are saltwater crocs, which can grow up to an impressive six metres, and whose diet includes wallabies, water-rats, birds, fish and snakes. A crocodile often attacks at water's edge, dragging its victim underwater until it drowns. Both crocodile species have tough, armoured skin, long, powerful tails and can be found in the north and north-east.

FROGS

There are five families of frogs in Australia, but there would only be four if the pestilent cane toad hadn't been introduced to Queensland in 1935. Apart from the cane toad, there are true frogs, tree frogs, southern frogs and narrow-mouthed frogs. Some species have proved remarkably adaptable: Australia's deserts are home to water-holding frogs that carry a store of water deep underground to last them in case of extreme drought.

POSSUMS

Possums are nocturnal creatures that have survived particularly well into the 20th century. With strong, handlike claws and a tail that serves as a fifth limb, brush-tailed possums are adept tree climbers and leapers who feed on leaves, fruit and blossoms and often make their homes in peoples' roofs. Like koalas, brush-tailed possums used to be hunted for fur. While brush-tailed possums are found all over Australia, the eastern pygmy possum lives in temperate rainforests, woodlands and heaths on the south-eastern mainland and in Tasmania. Eastern pygmy possums look like mice but, unlike mice, carry their young in a pouch.